DRAGONS IN AUTUMN

Laura Shenton

DRAGONS IN AUTUMN

Laura Shenton

Iridescent Toad Publishing

Iridescent Toad Publishing.

© Laura Shenton 2025
All rights reserved.

Laura Shenton asserts the moral right to be identified as the author of this work.

No part of this publication may be reproduced, stored or transmitted in any form or by any means, electronic, mechanical, photocopying, recording, scanning, or otherwise without written permission from the publisher. It is illegal to copy this book, post it to a website, or distribute it by any other means without permission.

All cover images used under a commercial license.

First edition. ISBN 978-1-913779-00-9

On autumn's edge, where shadows creep,
The dragon wakes from summer's sleep.
Nature moves without delay,
As foliage of bronze begins to sway.

The dragon walks through autumn's door,
Where rose-kissed skies are rich with lore.
It inhales deep the season's air,
And finds a world beyond compare.

Golden scales gleam in the autumn light,
Through burnished fragments, a dragon takes flight.
The atmosphere whispers secrets of old,
As ancient tales in flame unfold.

Among the fields where pumpkins rest,
Dragons revel in autumn's best.
Through tangled paths, the season's maze,
The creatures glide in playful craze.

Beneath red trees, a dragon rests,
Within the scene, its breath is blessed.
Smoke curls like tendrils through the air,
This autumn dusk is nature's fayre.

The forest simmers in muted hues,
As a dragon's roar echoes through the night.
Its wings, like embers, stir the breeze;
Autumn's shift is bound to please.

Through autumn's woods, where silhouettes play,
A dragon roams in soft decay.
Acorns drop and pinecones fall,
A whispered call to creatures small.

Each dragon scale, a work of art,
Like autumn leaves, no two the same.
A world of beauty, flame, and light,
In every pattern; never mundane.

Like saffron-veined remnants that fall in constant view,
Each dragon scale shines, so firm and true.
Each unique, yet all combine,
To craft a form both fierce and fine.

In twilight's hold, the dragon dreams,
Of harvest moons and flowing streams.
Her fire heats the chilling eve,
Among the trees that still believe.

Where mountains rise and valleys dip,
Dragons glide on autumn's grip.
Their every move, a frolic so pure,
With nature's rhythm, strong and sure.

Amber eyes in reflection glow,
As dragons watch the river flow.
The waning sun, so low and weak,
Embraces all in autumn's peak.

Tangerine flecks twirl a radiant dance,
The dragon moves as if in trance.
Its scales blend with colours of fall,
A creature grand, majestic, tall.

On the mountaintop, the dragon lies,
As autumn paints the evening skies.
The biting winds weave through its lair,
A season's end, both bleak and fair.

Crisp winds howl as dragons play,
In fields where once green meadows lay.
Their excitement ebbs the autumn dark,
A vital spark in every heart.

In autumn's lustre, the dragons greet,
Their laughter rising through the heat.
They teach the young to guard the flame,
Preparing for the cold's harsh claim.

The dragon's breath in morning mist,
Her scales a stunning amethyst.
She guards the forest, old and wise,
The season's gaze within her eyes.

A dragon's scales like flecks of gold,
Shimmer as the nights grow cold.
Autumn's hand has touched its wings,
And still the creature calmly sings.

The forest floor, the colour of flames,
Where dragons walk, they feel no shame.
In autumn's splendour, they find their peace,
Their love, their joy: it will not cease.

Beneath the harvest moon's full face,
The dragon dances with such grace.
Its fiery spray brightens the night,
Turning autumn's chill to a toasty delight.

By crackling flames of autumn's fire,
A dragon watches; he admires.
The bonfire's flicker, a kindred light,
Ignites him whole, a soothing sight.

In autumn's tenure, the dragon basks,
A time of rest its only task.
The trees bow low in silent praise,
For beings born of ancient days.

Through amber woods, where flavours blend,
Dragons taste the autumn trend.
Caramel and maple's charm,
Please their tongues with sweet, soft balm.

Like autumn quilts that catch the sun,
Each dragon scale is finely spun.
A world of colours, fierce and bright,
A blend of beauty, pure and right.

Through the fields of rust and red,
The dragon weaves, its hunger fed.
The autumn winds in sorrow sigh,
As the dragon's form consumes the sky.

On a sea of twigs, the dragon treads,
With careful steps where autumn spreads.
Its shadow stretches long and thin,
As autumn dusk comes creeping in.

The dragon's eyes, like pools of gold,
Reflect the autumn's tale, untold.
Its wings, like banners, sweep the ground,
A fleeting trace without a sound.

Autumn's mark upon the land,
Inspires the dragon: never bland.
With every leaf that tumbles down,
His scales will turn a richer brown.

In autumn's maze where corn stalks sway,
Dragons weave through paths that twist and play.
Their wings part fields in gentle breeze,
Unravelling secrets with practiced ease.

Through valleys rolling and mountains high,
A dragon soars the autumn sky.
The fading day upon its scales,
Tells stories old as ancient tales.

Through the orchard, a dragon glides,
Where apples fall and pleasure abides.
The scent of cinnamon fills the air,
As sumptuous pies are baked with flair.

Mist-shrouded peaks hide draconic lairs,
Flame-breath warms cooling stone.
Focused eyes gleam in nocturne's embrace,
Autumn's bounty sates reptilian appetite.

Through rustling woods and fields of grain,
A dragon soars with no refrain.
It chases echoes of a song,
Forgotten notes where solace belongs.

Wingbeats scatter fallen foliage,
Mountain caves beckon with promise of rest.
A dragon's hoard glints in the autumn sunset,
Scales shed among nature's fading palette.

In a cave of amber light,
The dragons love the cosy sight.
Around the fire, so hot and bright,
They welcome how it feels just right.

The elder dragons gather close,
Sharing heat as darkness grows.
Young ones learn from ancient lore,
Of how to keep the winter's roar.

The dragon's presence ignites the dark,
A fleeting flash, a sudden spark.
Autumn shards like embers fall,
As dragons rise at gloaming's call.

A dragon's tail sweeps through the leaves,
Creating paths where autumn grieves.
The forest bows to this great beast,
In autumn's grace, it finds its feast.

The sky is draped in hues of red,
As dragons stir upon their bed.
Their aura, just like autumn's breeze,
Sets the world at perfect ease.

From travel through a gracious flight,
The dragon families reunite.
They huddle close, ideas they share;
A new generation to prepare.

In autumn's haze, the dragon lies,
With vibrant embers in its eyes.
The world turns slow, the moment is still,
As nature bends to autumn's will.

The forest sings a quiet song,
Of dragons where the roots belong.
Their shadows, stretching long and lean,
As autumn crowns this mighty scene.

In the fading time of day,
The dragon sleeps, the skies turn grey.
Autumn's veil wraps round his form,
But still he doesn't fear the storm.

On the mountain, high and steep,
A dragon finds a place to sleep.
Autumn's hand will paint her dreams,
With flowing wisps and vibrant streams.

The leaves swirl down in fiery rain,
As dragons venture on textured terrain.
The elders teach with gentle fire,
As young ones gather to enquire.

A dragon's breath in autumn air,
Sends warmth to those who wander there.
Its eyes, like lanterns, guide the way,
No soul is ever left astray.

In autumn's spectrum, the dragon shines,
Each scale a jewel, so rare and fine.
Like leaves that flutter to the ground,
In every one, a joy is found.

The dragon's wings beat slow and true,
Through autumn skies of pink and blue.
The world below in shades of rust,
Rises in a cloud of dust.

In the forest, vast and wide,
The dragon makes his home inside.
Autumn's chill he does not fear,
Within him burns a fire so near.

Autumn's touch in every tree,
Reflected in its soul, so free.
The dragons gather in the wood,
To share the joy as old friends should.

As evening falls, the dragon sighs,
Breathing in the autumn skies.
Cinnamon scents from hearth to door,
As pumpkin spice is prepared once more.

The dragon's roar, a distant sound,
Echoes through the woods profound.
Vibrato ripples through the air,
As decibels shake everywhere.

In gorgeous twilight's gentle hue,
The dragon finds its rest anew.
Evening's zest upon its scales,
Will tell a tale that never pales.

The dragon's belly is full of fire,
As autumn winds do lift him higher.
Through the sky, he soars with pride,
A creature born to never hide.

In autumn's flurry, the dragons meet,
To share their warmth and stories sweet.
They speak of love and ancient lore,
Of autumns past and legends more.

In the valley, cool and deep,
The dragon finds a place to sleep.
Autumn's canopy around it falls,
A gentle blanket, covering all.

In autumn's heart, the dragon stays,
While aromas fill the crisp, cool days.
The warmth of pie, both sweet and spiced,
Is certainly a tempting vice.

On the edge of autumn's shore,
The dragon thrives forevermore.
It moves in silence through the wood,
A creature wise, a being good.

The season stokes ancient instincts,
Claws dig, sharp in softening soil.
Talons grasp at fall's last bounty,
Leathery hide must toughen for winter.

The dragon's roar splits the sky,
Sending smoke-brushed clouds awry.
Autumn's song in every cry,
As sundown cues a peaceful sigh.

The last leaf falls, the dragon lands,
In forests deep where time expands.
Its scales, as natural as the earth;
They complement the season's birth.

Leathery wings shroud harvested fields,
Claws scrape rock as rodents yield.
Scaled hides shimmer as groups encroach,
Dragons adapt for winter's approach.

In autumn's final, fleeting days,
A dragon dances through the haze.
Her fire blends with the dying light,
A soft farewell with winter in sight.

www.ingramcontent.com/pod-product-compliance
Lightning Source LLC
Chambersburg PA
CBHW030044100526
44590CB00011B/330